HOW TO TRAIN YOUR PET LIKE A TELEVISION STAR

BY RAY BERWICK

Second Printing, February 1978

Copyright ©1977 by Armstrong Publishing Company
Library of Congress Catalog Card Number: 77-83372

ISBN: 0-915936-06-2
Printed in the United States of America

Edited By:
Carl G. Armstrong and Florine Sikking

Designed By:
Augie Rinaldi

Published By:
Armstrong Publishing Company
5514 Wilshire Boulevard
Los Angeles, California 90036

June 2, 1977

This book is for anyone who loves animals — and that includes all of us.

I've been in front of the camera for thirty years working with animals since I was a kid and until I saw Ray handle his animals I never knew what it was all about. Always before it was chains, leashes, punishment, keep them hungry and keep them scared; but with Ray it's all love and reward. It works a thousand times better and it's a pleasure to be with a healthy, happy animal who loves people and enjoys being with them.

Ray also presents the only valid philosophy for saving our wild life — that being instead of creating a rigid line between civilization and wild life, he has the wisdom to suggest that we incorporate both. Indeed, there is no reason why a peregrine falcon can't roost on the top of the Black Tower at Universal, why we can't feed deer in our backyard and why all animals can't co-exist with us in the entire civilized world.

My hat's off to him for the work he's done for animals and for writing this book.

Sincerely,

ROBERT BLAKE
BARETTA

ABOUT THE AUTHOR

Ray Berwick is the Executive Producer of the Bird and Animal Shows at Universal Studio Tours and is acknowledged as the leading bird and animal trainer in both TV and the motion picture industry. His major movie credits include Alfred Hitchcock's thriller "The Birds," "Birdman of Alcatraz," "Jonathan Livingston Seagull," and "Eye of the Cat."

In the field of television, Mr. Berwick is responsible for training the bird and animal performers in a score of current TV commercials as well as many continuing television series. The personable cockatoo, Fred, on "Baretta" is one of Mr. Berwick's stars. Fred is the two-time winner of the coveted Grand Patsy Award as well as the Photoplay Award, "Most Popular Animal Actor." The television series "Little House on the Prairie" will feature one of the many actors from Mr. Berwick's stable, the dog Bandit.

In addition, Mr. Berwick is the Executive Producer of the Bird and Animal Shows at Lion Country Safari in Laguna Hills, California, San Diego Wild Animal Park and Marriott's "Great America Park" in Gurnee, Illinois.

Mr. Berwick resides in Sherman Oaks, California with his wife Suzanne and their poodle, Gaby.

TABLE OF CONTENTS

MOTION PICTURE AND TELEVISION TRAINED DOG

Hi! My name is Fred and I'm helping with this book: HOW TO TRAIN YOUR PET LIKE A TELEVISION STAR.

It's really not very hard at all. Who knows, your pet might get to be a great actor like me — even a television star.

First let's talk about your pet. The real trick is to train your pet and still be friends with him. I might as well warn you — this is going to take a little bit of patience and a little bit of love — maybe a whole lot of love.

Who would have thought when I landed here seven years ago I would wind up on television? Here's how it all happened: A bird exporter in Hong Kong, whose name I never did know, loaded me inside a big wire cage with a bunch of funny looking chickens and other strange birds.

Before I knew what was happening I was out over the ocean headed for California in these big United States. The truth is, at first I thought I was being eaten by some monstrous bird about eight million times as big as I am. I got a few good peeks at him when they stuffed me and the chickens in what appeared to be his mouth which was located, in of all places, right in the middle of his stomach.

I have always considered myself to be a pretty nifty flyer but right away I decided I wasn't even in it. That big rascal was flying like nothing I had ever seen. I could tell by the feel of it. He was flying faster than I had ever dreamed of. Not only that, he flew for hours without ever beating his wings. Something else I couldn't understand at the time. He had the loudest, noisiest stomach I had ever heard.

Of course, all this happened just a short time after I left the jungle. I was pretty dumb at the time. I wasn't even able to speak English. In Hong Kong I had picked up a few words in Chinese which I said over and over in several different kinds of voices.

That was seven years ago. I'm a lot smarter now. Now I know that wasn't a big bird at all but an airplane. I've flown on them many times since. The roaring sound that had my crest on end wasn't his stomach at all but four big super jet engines.

When the importer in Los Angeles, California, picked me and the chickens up at the airport he took one look inside the cage and said, "Man! you're some kind of funny lookin' chicken." He called Ray Berwick and asked him if he'd like to buy a weird chicken.

One thing I like about Ray, he's always willing to take a chance. Before long he and I were real buddies. He brought me right to Universal Studios where I've lived ever since. Sometimes I even feel like I run the place.

Like I say, Ray is a pretty good guy even if he can't fly a lick — like the old joke some talking birds use when talking to people — "I can talk. Can you fly?"

Naturally, I can do all that plus all kinds of tricks. I don't think Ray realized how good I actually was. Maybe he was just waiting for me to learn to speak English properly. In any case, we just buddied around for several months. I would perch on his hand while we roamed around the studio and talked to each other. I got to be a pretty lively conversationalist. I could answer almost any question I was asked. I was even able to ask a few of my own, like — "When do I join the act?"

That did it. I learned a routine quicker than you can shake a feather. Then I joined the ANIMAL ACTOR SHOW at UNIVERSAL STUDIO TOURS. If I must say so I was an instant hit. One thing had me puzzled. Ray never used me in a motion picture or a television show. He said he was saving me for the right one.

It didn't happen for another five years. One day Ray came in all excited. He said there was an interview for a mynah bird on a television series called BARETTA. "FRED," he smiled, "here's your big shot. I'm going to show our mynah bird HOWARD but I'm also going to show you. Don't blow it."

The three of us hustled down to the producer's office. About ten people gathered around. Ray put HOWARD'S cage on a desk. The big dope was leaping back and forth from one perch to another like a maniac. Suddenly, he squawked, "My name is HOWARD." Big deal. Then he started leaping back and forth again. Not very impressive. In fact, I was a little embarrassed for him.

Ray took me out of my cage and passed me to Robert Blake. "Mr. Blake," the producer announced, "will be playing the part of BARETTA." I took one look at Robert Blake and liked him instantly. He was my kind of man. He had guts.

I'm naturally outgoing so I wasn't the least bit nervous. Excited yes, but not nervous. Standing on Mr. Blake's arm I went into my routine and in ten seconds flat I had my audience in an uproar, laughing and applauding. Mr. Blake grinned while I gave him a kiss, waved, put my head against his chest to show him I loved him. Finally, I did my imitation of a barking dog and a crowing chicken. By this time he was laughing. He handed me back to Ray and stated flatly, "That's him. On this show we go with the talent."

The rest is history. The first years of BARETTA, Mr. Blake won the EMMY AWARD for the best television actor of the year and I won the GRAND PATSY AWARD (that's the award for the best animal actor of the year). Not only that, it was the first time in history that a single award had been given to include all categories. That means I was voted the best animal actor in any of the following: motion pictures, television or commercials. I have recently been informed that I have won the prestigious PHOTOPLAY AWARD for the best animal actor of the last ten years. The award will be presented on national television. I am one proud cockatoo.

That's about it. I've told you about myself. I want everybody to know I'm happy in my work. A bird like me, or any kind of an animal, can be trained and be happy at the same time. Happier, even than if he or she is not trained at all. It all depends on how it's done. Between you and me, I think Ray Berwick and I know more about training pets than anybody. We'll try to pass this knowledge on to you.

Think about this: besides being able to talk and do all kinds of tricks, I can ride my own bicycle (just my size), my own roller skates and my own scooter. Imagine all the fun I have. Besides, there are other advantages to being a cockatoo. I can live to be one hundred years old. If you'd like to teach your pet some of these things, get ready.

Ray Berwick
with
friends Punkin' and Jake

Ray's got a craggy looking face, right? Don't let that fool you. Inside he's got a heart of pure putty. He's a pussy cat. Maybe that's why we get along so well. I'm like that too, unless somebody tries to push me around.

Anyhow, Ray has been many things in his lifetime, a rodeo performer, a professional dancer, an actor and a writer. But always, he has had at least one pet as a special friend.

He has trained everything from a bull elephant to a humming bird. During the last twenty years he has spent full time training motion picture animals and birds. Here are just a few of his top credits: BIRDMAN OF ALCATRAZ with Burt Lancaster, Alfred Hitchcock's THE BIRDS, THE EYE OF THE CAT, SLAUGHTER HOUSE FIVE, THE SNOW GOOSE with Richard Harris, KING OF THE MOUNTAIN with Marlon Brando, THE LINDBERGH STORY with James Stewart, FRIENDLY PERSUASION and many many others.

He has had his animals and birds on almost all the major television series, including dogs, cats and birds on the LASSIE SERIES.

Currently, there is HENRY the Dog on EMERGENCY, BANDIT on LITTLE HOUSE ON THE PRAIRIE, and, of course, FRED the Cockatoo (that's me) on BARETTA.

Ray is located at Universal Studios. We have a live demonstration at UNIVERSAL STUDIO TOURS. We have other live shows at the SAN DIEGO WILD ANIMAL PARK, THE MARRIOTT'S GREAT AMERICA and LION COUNTRY SAFARI.

We've got a lot going on but we've got the best help love can buy. Our associates are the finest. You'll meet them later in this book. There is Bryan Renfro who helps tutor me, Greg Wallen who helps train everybody and watches after our health. There is Gary Price who, along with Greg, helps train Henry and has his own favorite bird named PEPPER. Like me, I sometimes think PEPPER is part human and we all sometimes think Gary is part bird. Then there is Steve Martin who trains and manages our Bird of Prey show in San Diego. Then there is a very fine gentleman named Robert Greenwood who takes me all over the country on personal appearance tours. Finally, the senior member of our group, Mr. Bob Branch. He manages our show at LION COUNTRY SAFARI. He looks exactly like Colonel Sanders and does a great job of selling our trained birds — alive, not fried.

That's the cast of characters. We all have the same philosophy — love is greater than the whip.

From here on I'll turn you over to my friend Ray. Good luck.

RAY BERWICK

Thank you, Fred. You're a mighty tough act to follow. All I can do is try.

I like what you said about having a trained pet and still having a friend. To us that's about the most important part. We don't mean to be sickening about it but if it takes severe punishment to train your pet, forget it. Speaking for ourselves, we have never resorted to cruelty to train one of our animals or birds.

We don't mean you should let your pet run the show. You should not only be his buddy but his boss, too. There is a way. We'll give you our ideas as we go along.

Since Fred is a bird and he has offered to pose for the training pictures, we might as well start with birds.

WHAT KIND OF A BIRD?

In case you don't already have one, think about what kind of bird you'd like to train. If you want one for a companion, here are some suggestions: a crow, raven, pigeon, chicken, duck, goose, sparrow, parakeet, canary, cockateel, parrot, macaw, cockatoo or almost anything else in the parrot family. Eagles, hawks and other birds of prey do not do well with parlor tricks but they too have their place. We'll tell you about them in another chapter.

One note of caution: if you're keeping any kind of wild bird as a pet, be sure to check with the local Fish and Wildlife Authorities to find out about the legal aspects.

HOW MUCH MONEY?

Normally, anything in the parrot family except for parakeets and cockateels will be quite expensive. It would not be too unusual to find price tags up to $300.00 for a parrot or $2,500.00 for a cockatoo.

There are all kinds of birds so you should be able to find one to suit you.

REMEMBER

Don't push your bird too fast. If he doesn't like you or what you have to offer, he will probably fly away. Most of the fun in training pets is learning to communicate and establish a firm base of love and understanding.

WHAT WE THINK IT'S ALL ABOUT

We train almost entirely on the theory of positive reinforcement. There are dozens of books you could read on that subject. In those books are hundreds of complicated words which could serve to confuse one utterly.

The whole thing is as simple as this: positive reinforcement, in the terms we use it, means that when you train your pet and he does something you want him to do, then you do something in return for him. It could mean just a friendly pat on the head. Usually it means something to eat. A treat. The treats should be in small bits so you only give a little bite at a time. Otherwise, very quickly your pet will be full and the training session will be over.

If at the end of the training session he has not had enough to eat, feed him whatever amount he needs from your hand. A good rule of thumb with a bird is to feel his breast bone (keel) and if it begins to feel sharp then he is not getting enough to eat.

THE CLICKER

When your pet does the trick you want him to, it is not always possible to give him his reward at that exact instant. What you do then is give him a "promise" by sounding the clicker. That will tell him that what he has just done has earned him a reward. Follow through. Give him his reward as soon as it is practical.

Animal behaviorists have many different kinds of sophisticated instruments for making sounds for reinforcement but none is any better than this simple clicker. It is easy to handle and has a very distinctive sound not easily mistaken for any other.

The clicker is a simple child's toy. Sometimes it is called a cricket. The sound is produced by pressing with your thumb. They can sometimes be bought in a toy department or in the party section of a department store.

Unfortunately, these toys are sometimes hard to find so we are providing one with each of our books.

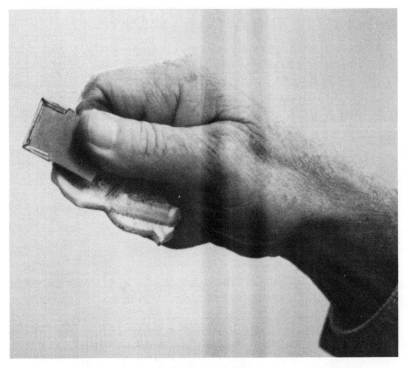

THE CLICKER

APOLOGY TO LIBERATED PETS

Miss, Mrs. and Ms. pets, please forgive us for referring to all pets as he. It's only to save time. We love you girls most of all.

LET'S
GET
STARTED

Fred is posing for the pictures as he promised so you can see we're giving it to you straight. He has one more word of advice. If your bird is a flyer and you want to let him fly later, you can put a little strip of tape around five or six outside feathers on one wing. This will keep him from flying very far until he gets used to being out of the cage. It may keep him from flying away or banging into something and injuring himself.

You may also clip the feathers of one wing but then you'll have to wait for a molt until he can fly again.

FIRST

You take your bird's feed out of his cage in the late afternoon. If he is a young bird, be sure to wait until he's eating well on his own.

The next day, when you think he's hungry, it's time to start. If you're right handed hold some seeds, or whatever treat you want to use, in that hand. If you're left handed do just the opposite.

Stick your hand with the treats inside the cage and let him eat from it. The cage in the picture is just a prop. Fred owns one that's quite fancy with a star on the door.

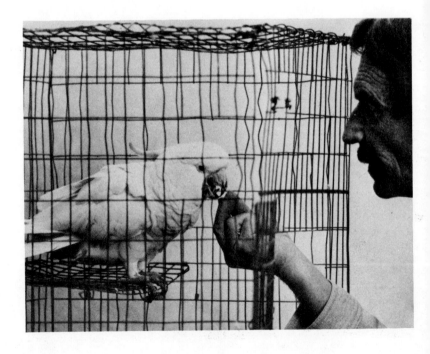

If he goes for the treats right away, he should step on your hand and continue to eat. When he does this, hold your other hand between the one with the treats and the bird. The idea is to have him stand on one hand and eat from the other. It may take a little time for him to learn to stay on the other hand, but stick with it. He will learn.

When this is going well, very gently take hold of the talons of the foot nearest your fingers. Very gently. He may not like this at first but he will get used to it as he continues to eat.

When he has reached this point, close the hand holding the treats and start feeding one treat at a time.

These important steps allow you to control the length of the training period.

When the bird is calm and no longer afraid, very carefully take him out of the cage. Watch for him to try to fly away the first time or two. He will be excited at being outside the cage.

Most birds are smarter than you think and very soon will begin to enjoy this relationship. If you treat your pet with kindness you should have a friend for life.

BARETTA AND FRED

BARETTA AND FRED

TIME FOR THE CLICKER

When your bird has learned to sit on your hand, find him a suitable perch. When he is relaxed on that, push your hand against his chest and make him step back on your hand. The instant he does, click the clicker and give him his treat. Keep it up until he is ready to get on your hand as soon as it is near.

Besides using the clicker, we like to talk to our pets and praise them as much as possible when they are doing well. You can call him to you with whichever words you like, but try to stay consistent so that he learns certain words for certain behaviors. You will be amazed at how soon he may learn the meaning of different words and expressions.

For every signal you give with your hand, there should be corresponding words. Eventually, he should learn to react to either one.

By the same token, he should learn the meaning of the word "NO." There will be times when it's needed — like when he gives you a nip, or at another time when he has one idea and you have another.

On the following pages are the steps in learning to fly to your hand. If your bird's wings aren't clipped, we think this aspect of training is very important.

Your bird may love you very much and want to be with you whenever he can. Still, if he is out in the open and should get frightened he might fly off. For some strange reason an inexperienced bird will become very frightened when he first flies all on his own in the big world outside. He may land in a tree and want desperately to come down to your hand but not actually know how. Unless he has learned this well before then he could well be lost for good.

On the following pages are illustrations of the way it's done. First, a short jump. The next one a little farther. Before he is taken outside without a taped wing he should be ready to come to you from any distance.

THE FLIGHT

Your bird has already learned to step on your hand for a treat. Now, back your hand away far enough so that he cannot step to it. Coax him by showing him the treat. The first big jump is the hardest. Reinforce each jump with the sound of the clicker.

1.

THEN A LITTLE FARTHER

It should be easier now and he will begin to join in the fun.

2.

FROM A DISTANCE

By this time he will be in the spirit of the game. If everything has gone right, he will most likely fly to you from any distance just for the fun of a free ride.

3.

READY FOR THE NEXT ONE

You might start teaching him to give you a kiss. With this one, you must be the judge. If your bird is bad tempered by nature, you might want to pass.

Hold a treat close to your face. Watch his reactions closely. He might still be afraid of being too close to your face. That could make him give you a painful nip. It may be that he is still frightened and needs more handling. Like we say, you will have to be the judge. If he is frightened, be cautious and take it in gradual stages.

HERE WE GO

If you think he's relaxed and it's safe, keep moving the treat closer to your mouth. When you're sure all's well put the treat between your lips and let him take it by himself. The instant he does, sound the clicker and give him another treat from your hand. Continue doing this until he reaches for the treat without hesitation. Remember, be sure to give him a treat from your hand each time.

THE FIRST KISS

Now, when everything is going well and he is taking the treat every time, it's time for a trick of your own.

The next time he reaches for the treat, be ready. Just before he touches you with his beak draw the treat inside your mouth with your lips; sound the clicker and quickly give him the reward from your hand.

For this training, we use sunflower seeds. It's easier that way.

If it doesn't work right away, you may have to back up and let him take the treat from your lips a few more times.

HE LOVES YOU

This is the one we like. He puts his head against your chest to show affection.

Start by making him take the treat very close to your chest. Hold the treat in such a way he has to turn his head to get it.

Each time he takes the treat from this position, you, of course, sound the clicker and give him another one from your hand but away from your chest.

When he is placing his head against you properly, begin to hold the treat longer to keep him in that position.

Finally, when he puts his head against you with no help from you, start moving your hand away as I am doing in the picture.

He should learn to hold that position until you sound the clicker or indicate otherwise that he has done what you wanted.

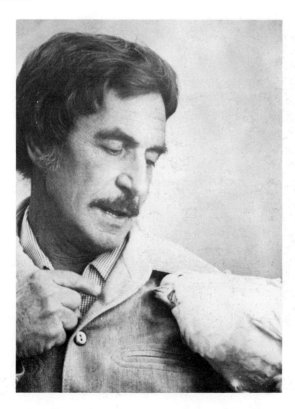

TEACH HIM TO WAVE

Set him on his perch. Hold your finger or a small stick near his foot, tempting him to reach for it. You might even touch the foot but don't actually let him take hold. When he does lift his foot, immediately sound the clicker and reward him.

As he begins getting the idea, move your finger or the stick farther away. Move it up and down, encouraging him to follow the same movement. At the same time use the word "WAVE." He should learn to wave as you see Fred doing.

TAKE A BOW OR NOD HIS HEAD "YES"

He can learn this one whether or not he has learned to fly to your arm.

Hold your arm a short distance away and encourage him to come to the treat. The instant he bends down to take off, sound the clicker and give the reward. The trick is to sound the clicker and reward him before he can fly away. By this time, he should know the sound of the clicker means he has done the right thing. As quickly as possible eliminate the arm posture altogether by lowering your arm a little each time.

The cue he should learn to recognize is your pointed finger of the opposite hand.

SHAKE HIS HEAD "NO"

You will notice how the more your bird learns the easier it is for him to pick up the next trick.

Shaking the head "NO," may work two ways.

First, try blowing his neck feathers to make them ruffle. Most likely he will shake his head instinctively. Catch him with the clicker when he does. By now he knows what that means.

The other trick is to stick a tiny piece of tape on the back of his head. When he tries to shake it off reinforce with clicker and reward. Use the word "NO," each time so he learns that as a cue. The hand cue our birds learn to recognize is simply holding the hands together as though shaking your own hand.

ON HIS BACK

It's unnatural for any bird to lie on its back. Yet, they will do it willingly and even enjoy it if they are confident of their master. Most of them will learn; gentle handling is the key.

When the bird is relaxed, try stroking his back and head gently. If he has any objections overcome them by giving him a reward each time. Before long his fear of being touched on the back should disappear and he will even like being scratched under the feathers.

Gradually, start holding the one hand across his back more firmly as he stands on the other hand. Begin to tilt him over a little at a time. Don't go too far without giving him a reward as you straighten him up.

Both of your hands will be occupied so it helps if you can get another person to give the treats when he is in a tilted position.

When he is lying on his back in your hand, the other hand will be free to feed him.

You may have a small amount of trouble getting this hand free. He will want to hold it with his talons for security. He will want to hold on to something. Push his feet together and he will lock them together and your hand will be free.

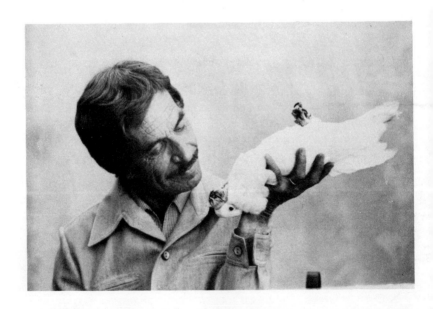

THIS TAKES CONFIDENCE

RETRIEVE

How about having the fastest delivery service in town? You've got it. Just follow the clues and you'll have a great show-off trick for your friends. It will take a little dedication on the part of both you and the bird.

Following the sequence as illustrated by Bryan Refro and Fred, here's how it works:

Have the clicker ready in one hand. Pick an object the bird is capable of carrying and touch it to his beak. Click and reward. Do this a few times until he gets the connection between the object and the reward. Then:

Hold the object to his beak and wait for him to make a move. When the click and reward is not forthcoming he will want to know what's happening. If he doesn't take hold of it on his own, move it around slightly until he does. You know what happens now. The instant he takes it in his beak, the click and reward.

IT'S BEGINNING TO WORK

Make him hold the object a little longer each time by delaying the reinforcement. By this time, we know you're learning the technique. Most all behaviors are trained in stages; one step at a time. The good part is that after a while your pet will begin trying his best to understand exactly what you want him to do and will be anxious to grasp each behavior as soon as possible.

If he's pretty smart, and most birds are, his understanding may reach the point where he will learn something new the first time.

PLACEMENT

Once he learns to hold an object, he then should learn to bring it to you. This is best accomplished by first teaching him to put the object in a container of some kind such as you see in the picture.

Occasionally, a bird will learn to place the object in your hand right away. If that's the case you may delete the container.

Normally, he will learn to make the placement to a container much quicker. After he learns it that way, it's easy to make the transfer to your hand by simply holding your hand over the container and taking the object from him.

The demonstration here is with the use of a container. When he has taken the object, place the container directly under it. Wait until he drops it in the container and reinforce with a reward. Soon he will get the idea — the object must be dropped in the container for him to collect. Move the container away from him gradually.

LOOK MOM NO HANDS

In the two pictures below you will note that FRED has learned to pick the object up and take it to the container. Pretty smart fellow don't you think? No wonder he's such a ham.

NOW HE'S REALLY COOKING

The sequence of training has been gradual but by this time your pet, like FRED, should be able to pick up an object and fly with it to one arm and place it in the other hand. If he's really on the ball, the distance won't be a big factor. For reasons of practical photography the flying distances shown in the pictures are quite short. However, he will perform the same way from distances up to one hundred feet and more.

After he is proficient, the retrieved object may be changed simply by showing him the new object and asking him to pick it up.

By using the retrieve, you may show some very impressive stunts like sending him to get the keys out of your car or almost anything else your imagination can come up with.

Here are some of FRED'S special toys, his bicycle, scooter and skates. He can actually ride them very well.
Unless you're a real buff we don't recommend them.
They're more expensive than people ones.

TALENTED MACAW

DEAD BIRD

Here is associate Gary Price with one of our favorite birds named PEPPER. He is demonstrating his dead bird act. When Gary says "DEAD BIRD!" PEPPER'S head drops.

STANDING ON HEAD

Here PEPPER demonstrates standing on his head. In training, he was simply placed in that position and reinforced a number of times until he learned to do it by himself.

Some of these tricks which look seemingly impossible are actually very easy for the bird to learn. After the kind of training we have described with FRED, your bird is ready for almost anything. Many times they will learn a new trick in a matter of minutes.

By using the clicker and food reinforcement as we have described, the sky is the limit. Your bird can learn very nearly any trick of which he is physically capable. It all depends on your own patience and ingenuity.

Here is one of our trained crows by the name of JOEY, demonstrating he, as well as many other kinds of birds, can learn the finer points.

ALFRED HITCHCOCK and one of our birds from "THE BIRDS."

From left to right: **SAMANTHA** the goose from
FRIENDLY PERSUASION, FRED, BABY the eagle featured
with **ANDY GRIFFITH** in **EAGLE ONE** as well as **KODAK
COMMERCIALS** and many others.

Trainer, **STEVE MARTIN** with one of our trained hawks at the **SAN DIEGO WILD ANIMAL PARK.**

Trained raven, JO JO, also at the SAN DIEGO WILD ANIMAL PARK.

MARY TYLER MOORE with AMIGO the toucan from WHAT'S SO BAD ABOUT FEELING GOOD.

CHARLTON HESTON with one of our red tail hawks from **WARLORD.**

PUNKIN', my favorite raven of all times with LASSIE.

RAVENS AND CROWS

These birds can be trained in almost exactly the same way as we have recommended for the other birds. The main difference is the diet. They are, for the most part, meat eaters so the best kind of treats would be ground meat or possibly dog kibble.

Remember, these birds are notorious thieves. If you aren't careful, your bird will try to grab all the treats at one time and the training session will be over.

Again, be sure to check with the local Fish and Wildlife Authorities regarding the law.

HAWKS, EAGLES AND OTHER RAPTORS

Historically, birds in this category have been used for hunting and falconry. In that respect, they are trained to do what they would normally do in a wild environment. The difference is that as "manned falcons" they are subject to the presence and direction of a human.

We have trained many of these birds for falconry and there are many published books dealing with the sport. We cannot allow ourselves the luxury of dealing with all the details. Such books are available at the library and at many book stores.

In our opinion there is another and much more exciting sport for these birds. You can have the thrill of a lifetime without worrying about the season or hunting laws.

In some states the possession of any bird of prey is illegal. In others it is not. It depends on where you live. The question can be answered by asking your local Fish and Game Warden. You will need a permit from him and there are certain rules and regulations.

THE BIG THRILL

It is usually better to acquire a raptor at a young age although this is one of the few birds that will tame down and work for you even though he was trapped as an adult. If you are really interested, do a quick study with one of the falconry books and it will explain how to acquire your bird. It will also tell you how to fit him with "jesse's" (leather thongs on his legs) and what kind of feeding he requires.

If you want to know how to have the most fun and excitement read on: we suggest you try to get a *red tail hawk.* They are the easiest to come by and the best for the sport we will be talking about.

When you have trained your bird to fly to your fist when he is flying free, and you are confident he will respond to your whistle or call, you are ready.

Take him to a nearby hill or even a flat area if there is a gentle wind and the thermals are rising.

It is helpful to have two people but not absolutely essential. If there are two, one of you may hold the bird on his fist at the base of the windy side of the hill. The other party should move away from the bird on the side of the hill, being sure the bird can keep him in view. This means the breeze or thermal is rising up the side of the hill. The party with the bird should set him gently on the ground or a rock where he can see and hear the other person.

When this second person whistles and calls the bird he should react by starting in that direction cross wind. At first he will probably try to make a direct flight.

After a time, the hawk will learn it is easier to ride the updraft to the top of the hill and soar to the target where he can dive (stoop) to the protected fist. It is a beautiful and thrilling sight.

Hawks, according to some authorities, have been clocked in a stoop up to speeds of over a hundred miles per hour. To many falconers this will sound strange because they sometimes think of only falcons having a swift stoop.

I assure you red tail hawks have a tremendous stoop which, to me, is more spectacular than a falcon's.

If one pursues this training, the hawk will learn to go up one or two thousand feet when weather conditions are right. When he stoops straight down from that elevation it is really something to see. Red tails rarely come in slow but will smash into the fist where the bait is waiting.

One variation of this sport is to move farther and farther away from the release point. It will cause the bird to soar higher to look for you.

We have had them soar out of sight many times and not seen them again until they are stooping straight down.

Their eyesight is unbelievable and we have had them soar up and find us from a distance of ten miles away.

ABOUT FEEDING RAPTORS

We prefer not to feed our raptors live food. When working on his high flights, he will not be tempted to go hunting on his own unless he has been fed live game.

A FEW LAST WORDS ABOUT FEEDING BIRDS

When we are working our birds (any kind) we keep a weight chart on them. We use gram scales and they are quite expensive.

If you don't want to get this deeply involved, there is a good rule of thumb. Feel your bird's breast bone (keel). If it is sharp and prominent he is not getting enough to eat. When working, a bird should be slightly hungry but not to the extent it affects his health.

If for any reason he stops eating or looks overly droopy or if he is picky with his food, consult a veterinarian.

A HARRIS HAWK

They are considered to be the most intelligent of all the hawks.

HOW TO TRAIN YOUR DOG AND STILL BE HIS FRIEND

What can we say about dogs that hasn't already been said. We love them all. Working with them and training them day after day has proved their trust and love.

In turn, we do our utmost to treat them with love and respect. We think this philosophy is reflected in our training methods.

There are many books dealing with the training of dogs. Some of them we do not agree with. We do not believe in unusually rough and severe treatment. We feel that interaction between a dog and his trainer should be a two-way street. The dog should enjoy the training experience as well as the trainer.

There is sometimes a temptation to get too severe when frustration sets in. The trainer and the dog are both unhappy if tempers get out of hand.

If a dog is performing out of fear of a beating it will most certainly be evident. If he has an unusually strong heart he may just appear very mechanical. If undue punishment is used in training, the stress signs will surface in one way or another.

If we did not feel so strongly about such training there are still other considerations. Our dogs would do very poorly in front of a camera if they were wearing a cowed look and had their tails between their legs.

We do not say that a dog should not be made to mind. We do say there is a sensible way it can be done.

Our entire staff is dedicated to the idea that if an animal is trained and handled properly there is almost no limit to what it can learn. There is no limit to what a trainer can learn about his dog, as well.

With love and understanding we are convinced that a line of communication between a person and an animal can be developed that borders on mental telepathy.

During any uncomfortable period of training, when your dog is learning, a certain measure of discipline can be used. It can be firm but with a gentle touch. When he does understand what you're trying to put across don't be afraid to praise him and play with him a little bit to take away the sting.

Don't be discouraged if your dog doesn't seem to be learning anything in a particular session. It is a strange phenomenon that the training a dog has in one session often does not appear until the next session.

WHAT KIND OF A DOG?
MUTT OR PUREBRED?

Purebred dogs usually cost a lot of money. Many of them are well worth it. Additionally, you will have a pretty good idea of what your dog will look like when he's grown.

But, mutts can be rescued from the pound. If what you want is a dog to train and the love it can give you, why not save yourself some money and maybe save some poor pup from being put to sleep.

No one has ever proved to me a purebred dog is smarter than a mutt.

WHAT AGE TO START

There is a tremendous latitude regarding the time a dog can start to learn. They can be started from three months to five years old.

The ideal time for them to begin is from four months to one year old.

We have trained dogs that were quite old for some specific purpose but generally speaking by that time they have lost most of their enthusiasm and it seems a hardship for them to put out a great deal of energy.

HERE GOES

We will leave the straight obedience training to the other guys. Your dog will learn to mind and do more tricks and you both will enjoy it. Just hang in there and you and your dog will be able to do a one-man-one-dog show.

LEASH TRAINING

Leash control is first. In training a dog the leash is like the throttle and brakes rolled into one. He first learns to walk at your side without pulling off in another direction. This is the first use of the leash.

When restraining him do not let him keep a steady pull. He will become accustomed to that and come to believe it's the normal state of affairs. Instead of pulling him back into position, give him a fair yank and then leave the leash slack until you need to do it again. When you bring him into position, you can use the term "HEEL." What you are trying to put across is the idea that there is no stress on the leash when he is in position.

This part of training is critical. It is the time when the basic relationship is being established. Until now your dog has been doing mostly what he wanted to when he wanted to. For the first time he is learning to take direction. He may not like it at first. Be friendly but firm. After you have positioned him back at your side a few times, stop and pet him.

Let him know you're still his pal but you're his boss as well.

Since this stage determines who's training who, we suggest you stay with it for a long enough time to make certain the proper pattern is set. It may take two days or it may take two weeks but it is important.

We'd like you to meet our friend BANDIT, he is now a regular cast member of THE LITTLE HOUSE ON THE PRAIRIE T.V. series. He is a border collie and one of our best trained dogs and he will be posing for the pictures. When I brought him out on the leash he must have thought I had lost my mind. He hasn't had to use one in years. Then, when I started him on basic training he knew I had lost my mind.

When you stop, you may want your dog to sit. We do not train this stop-sit sequence in motion picture work because it is almost always what the director does not want. We train the "SIT" cue as a separate behavior. That will come a little later.

It would be good, however, to introduce two other very important commands: "NO!" and "STAY!" If he jumps up on you or starts sniffing a tree, restrain him with the leash and use the word "NO!" firmly but kindly. It is a word he must learn to understand.

The word "STAY!" is of equal importance. When you stop, make him stay in position. You may keep him at your left side and conform to obedience procedure if you like. Again, in motion picture training this is another thing we avoid. If the dog is constantly at the left side the obedience aspect is obvious.

We hope you are still using the leash. It will be with you for a while if you want a well trained dog. When you feel your dog has learned his first basic commands well enough, it's time to go on.

SAVE YOUR BACK

As the picture indicates, your dog is on a table about waist high. It need not be a table but anything to suit your own height.

It will help you in two ways. It keeps your dog in a close position and will certainly save a good many backaches. Also, it brings you both eye to eye where you are in a better position to determine when he is actually understanding the word cues.

Be sure the table is steady and doesn't wobble. If it does, he will most certainly lose confidence in both you and himself. Even when the table is steady, it will take him a little time to get used to it.

BANDIT is demonstrating a first lesson in SIT AND STAY. He is being held with the leash while one hand is used to push his rump into position. Now is the time you can start using treats.

TREATS — WE PART COMPANY WITH OTHER TRAINING METHODS

It's true. Most other training methods do not advocate using treats for training. We do. In fact, we think we can prove that a dog will learn more, and quicker, than by any other method. Later, if you want to eliminate treats and substitute a pat on the head, that's okay. In the meantime, stay with us. Your dog will learn more words and more behaviors in a shorter space of time than you would have believed possible. Also, we can eliminate most of the harsh discipline along the way.

WHAT KIND OF TREATS?

Treats can be anything your dog seems to have a preference for such as dog biscuits, weenies, ground meat, stewing beef or almost anything else that is handy and healthy. If dog biscuits or another dry food is used it should be broken into small bits so the dog doesn't get filled too quickly. If you use ground meat give small pinches. Any other kind of meat can be diced and fed either raw or cooked.

CLICKER

We usually don't use the clicker with dogs. We want them to learn as many words as possible so instead of the clicker we say "GOOD BOY" or which ever words fit the situation.

At this point, BANDIT has learned to sit without the hand making contact. The same motion you used in reaching for his rump becomes the hand cue along with the word itself. He should learn to respond to either one. In the beginning the words should be "SIT," and "STAY" if necessary. Reinforce either of these commands with a slight yank on the leash as a reminder.

PAY OFF TIME

The first few times he does the behavior properly, make him feel pleased with himself by praising him. At the same time give him the treat. The completion of the behavior and the treat with praise should be as closely connected as possible. It will make him start to listen and do his best to understand the command in order to earn the treat.

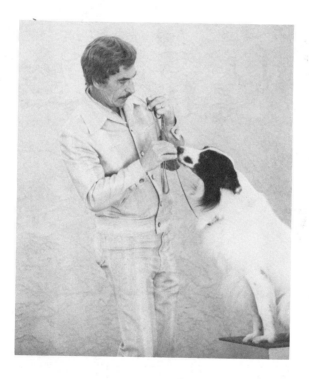

He has learned to sit but he must have a cue to stand. There is no way to properly exercise one behavior without the other.

STAND-STAY

The direct cue for STAND is a slight pull straight back on the leash as though you were going to lead him.
It does not always work, especially when he's on the table.

We prefer to stay close to the dog still on the table.
We pull the leash with one hand and touch, or lift him under the midsection or near the flank; at the same time saying the word "STAND."

As he begins to learn and you move farther away from the dog, the hand signal is done with the hand you were using to pull the leash, doing the motion but not actually putting pressure on the leash.

When your dog demonstrates he has a reasonable understanding of the three commands SIT! STAND! and STAY! he should have also learned the connection between getting his reward for having done the right thing. If things have gone well he will be listening and trying to cooperate. Continue the reward, petting and praising, but:

Now you begin keeping him in each position for a longer period of time by withholding the reward. When he does get it he should still be in position. And after the reward insist he remain in position until the next command or until he is released with a word or a signal.

THE HAND CUE FOR STAY

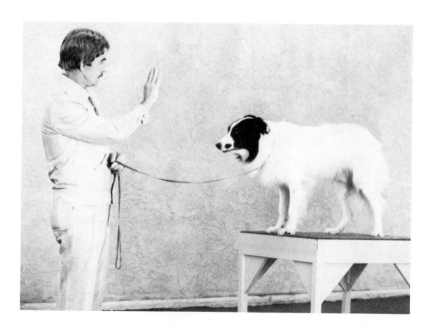

DOWN-STAY

From either a standing or sitting position, put one hand on the dog's head and push down. Pull the leash down with the other hand. The word cue is, of course, "DOWN." Both hands work together until he is all the way down as the picture shows.

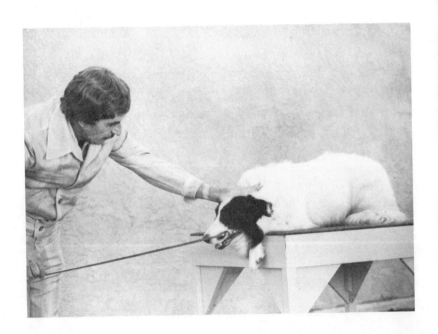

HAND CUE FOR DOWN

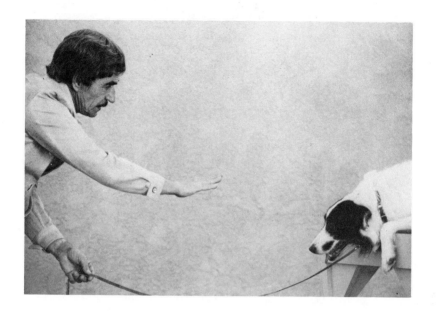

SOLID FUNDAMENTALS

These four commands are basic fundamentals. It is necessary that he knows them well. Almost everything that comes later involves one of them.

It's time now to start separating hand cues from word cues. He should learn them both well enough to respond separately to either one.

To sharpen him even more, stay close and begin using word cues only. If he doesn't fully understand a word add the hand signal.

Keep this exercise going until there's no doubt in your mind he has learned the words.

If he is slow and confused on any single word concentrate on it by going from one command to another and only rewarding the one he is weak on.

As you continue, keep in mind that all hand signals should appear to the dog to be the same motion you used when making physical contact.

VARIABLE REINFORCEMENT

The term simply means a treat is not offered for every behavior but is given at random intervals. He will still give his all for each trick, not being sure which one rings the bell.

TAKE A BREAK

In the first stages of training practice only from fifteen minutes to one half hour at a time. Even in advanced training, the sessions should not be extended much more than that. You may, however, work him a number of times in one day.

A good plan is to put him back in the house or kennel if you intend to work him again soon. He will be glad to get out again and will enter into the spirit of the project with much more enthusiasm.

STAY WITH THE LEASH

It may be a temptation to start working your dog off leash. We advise against it. There's still plenty of time for that. The longer you stay with the leash while he's still learning, the less chance of him breaking away in confusion.

If during this time he is allowed to make an independent decision and either quit or run, it makes future training much more difficult.

A good rule even with well trained dogs is to use a leash when beginning a new behavior.

OFF THE TABLE

At this time we think it's a good idea to leave the table for a short time so the pupil does not come to believe it's the normal way of life. In a matter of minutes he should be able to do all the things on the ground he has learned on the table.

RECALL

There are many more things to be learned off the table but for now we suggest only one new one. The recall. It will mean putting your dog in any of the positions he has learned and calling him to you.

Most likely he will come immediately but the trick is to keep him in position until you do call. If he tries to break too soon, insist he stay in position. You may once again have to reinforce the word STAY. You might have to do this by using a long cord or rope. It would be attached to his collar and strung around something behind him. The picture is this: the cord goes behind the dog, is strung around an upright object such as a post or rail. It then comes back past the dog to where you are holding the other end and facing the dog. If he starts too soon, you can hold him in position by keeping the cord tight.

If, on the other hand, he is reluctant to come to you, you may have to use his leash as well to urge him toward you. In this way you have control in both directions .

While you're at it, have him stop at different points between you and the starting position by giving the STAY signal. It will be excellent training. He will learn to mind while still a distance away and you will have control with the line. You should be able to dispense with the line in a relatively short time.

BACK TO THE TABLE — WAVE

This is an effective trick, one which is normally quite easy to teach. Your dog will be in a sitting position. Touch one of his paws until he lifts it up. Reward him quickly. Continue until he will lift the paw without you touching him. Begin to withhold the reward and move your hand up and down in a waving motion until he tries the same thing. He will be reaching out trying to touch your hand. Again, reward him with praise and a treat. He should get the idea fairly quickly. The verbal cue is "WAVE."

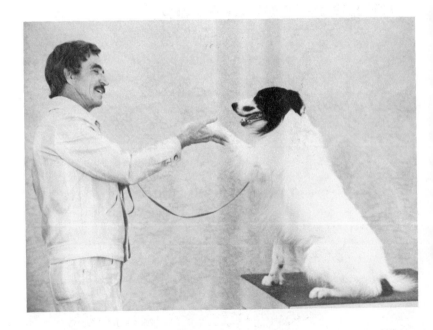

THE FINISHED PRODUCT

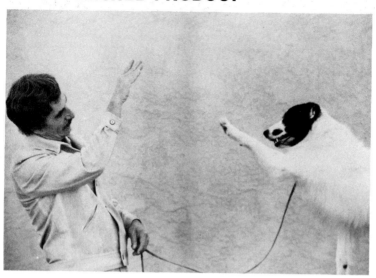

ON HIS SIDE OR DEAD DOG

When he is in a down position push him onto his side using the words "ON YOUR SIDE" or "DEAD DOG." The same motion you're using to push becomes the cue.

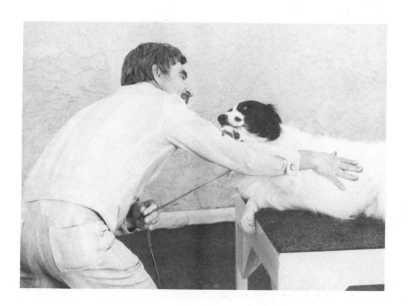

NOW ON CUE

SIT UP

This is best taught by having your dog in a corner or a place where he is supported and won't fall over backward. You first lift his chin or his paws. Hold him in that position and reward him. When he learns to stay put, make the motion of your hand more exaggerated as you lift his chin. He will learn to sit up when he sees the hand coming. As you move away from him, the same gesture becomes the hand cue. Move him away from the corner gradually when he learns to balance himself.

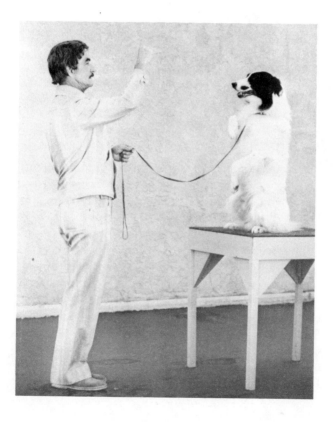

RETRIEVE

There is no quick way we know of for a dog to learn a good solid retrieve. Many dogs fetch in a spirit of play. The only problem with that is they will do it only when they feel like it. A ball-happy dog may fetch a ball for hours but give him a strange article and tell him to carry it along at your side and the whole thing is all over.

A desirable retrieve is one where a dog will pick up any article you tell him to and do with it what you tell him. To get this kind of result it must almost surely be a trained behavior.

A standard wooden dumbbell may be used. A glove, a rolled up newspaper or even a piece of cloth will do just as well.

THE FIRST STEP

First you hold the object up to the dog's muzzle and as gently as possible force it into his mouth. Here a battle of wills is sure to take place. He will immediately attempt to spit it out. Your job is to keep it there and say "HOLD IT." The battle is joined. He may twist and turn but make him hold it for at least a few seconds. Then make a point of taking the object out of his mouth yourself rather than letting him drop it. Use the word "OUT." Even though he has given you nothing but resistance, pet and praise him.

For a time it may be discouraging, but keep it up. When he finally holds the object a few seconds without your hand over his muzzle, praise him and make him feel like he's just won the best of show and at the same time give him a treat. Each time you force the object into his mouth use the words "PICK IT UP."

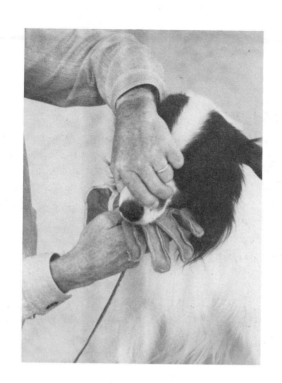

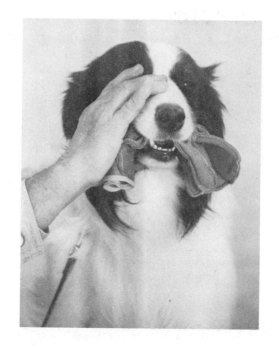

IT FINALLY HAPPENS

Don't expect it to happen the first session but eventually he will reach for the object all on his own. When he does, be perfectly still. Let him hold it only a short time and take it out of his mouth before he drops it. Let him know by praise and reward, he has done something extra special.

The next time, let him hold it a little longer but always try to take it before he drops it.

Start holding the object nearer the floor, making him reach down. Make him hold it longer each time.

You will note how even when you're holding the object at floor level he will, at first, not pick it up unless your hand is there. This is all a part of the gradualism connected with training this particular behavior. I have seen other trainers accomplish it in a shorter space of time by sheer brutality, by twisting the dog's ear or jowl until he opens his mouth to pick it up and twisting again if he drops it. We're against it. We'd rather take a little longer and do it right.

As you progress, you may give his leash a little yank to remind him of the business at hand.

When he has learned to pick it up you still have one more hurdle. When you call him to you, he will most surely drop it. This is best overcome by staying in quite close and using the leash. Don't use your voice to call him but pull him toward you just a short distance and keep repeating the words "HOLD IT." He should learn your intentions fairly soon as he puts the object in your hand. When this happens start moving farther away. Then start tossing the object a few feet away from him. Tell him to stay until the command: "PICK IT UP!" This is the point where all you and he have done becomes worthwhile. He will realize suddenly it's, after all, a pretty good game and will bounce to do his job when you give the command.

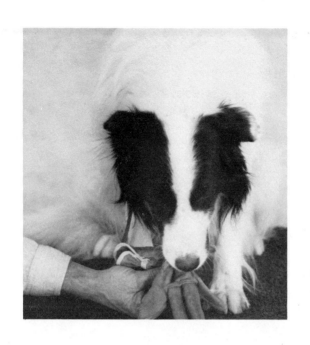

One of our dogs named JOHNNY who is familiar on TV.

TWO IN ONE

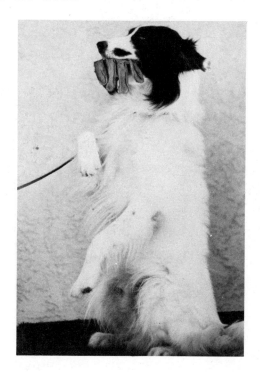

BANDIT is one of our prize possessions. We think he is living proof that our system of training is the right one. In any case, for us it is.

BANDIT is nine years old and does several shows per day at the Universal Tour demonstration. His enthusiasm never wavers. Even on hot uncomfortable days he goes through his routine like it's the very first time. He is a healthy and happy dog with a heart full of love for everybody.

THE SPEAK

Your task with this one is to train your dog to speak without crowding toward you at the same time. They all seem to want to do it in the beginning.

As you see in the picture, tie him off and stand a few feet away. Show him a treat and hold it about shoulder high. Tease him with it by moving your hand back and forth. Use the word "SPEAK!"

He should start bouncing around and get pretty excited, attempting to get to you and the treat. When this happens and he barks just once or even gives a little yip, rush to him and give praise and reward. Show enthusiasm and try the same thing again.

Each time make him come on a little stronger until he is giving you a full-fledged bark.

In time you should achieve the results of either wiggling the finger on hand cue or simply using the word "SPEAK."

Some dogs have a hard time getting the idea but most don't. If you have trouble, try walking away a good distance and ignore him. At some point, he will probably give a yip to get your attention. Pay him off quickly and try the same thing again but this time give him a little encouragement. If that doesn't work try any other ploy you can think of like playing with another dog where he can watch. Anything that gets him started is okay. Once it happens you can develop it further with the proper reinforcement.

WHEN HE HAS A GOOD SPEAK

You will want him to speak without crowding in close to your feet.

Make him sit or stand a few feet away. Give him the STAY command followed by the cue for speak. Walk to him to give the reward. If you call him to you during this training, he will want to keep cheating by moving forward.

This is a good time to review all the things he has learned by mixing them up, making him do his full bag of tricks at random so they do not become a routine.

If he is weak on any of them concentrate on that department by increasing the rewards for that particular behavior and decreasing it for others.

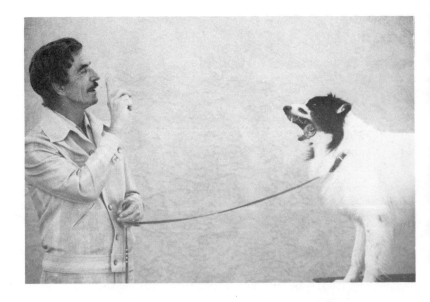

WALK ON HIS HIND LEGS?

We seldom teach a dog this trick for two reasons. It is bad for some dog's back legs and most dogs will use it as a cop-out when they are frustrated or don't want to do something else. But here's how it's done:

Start the dog in a sit up position. Hold a treat over his head and help him to his hind legs with the leash. Make him come to you only a couple of steps in the beginning and increase the distance as he becomes more proficient. The hand signal is the same as you started by holding the treat.

BACK UP

This is not a spectacular trick but a behavior which is very useful when you want to keep your dog in position or move him away from you.

Move toward him until he is crowded backward. As soon as he has taken the first backward step give him a treat. The hand motion is just as though you were pushing him away with the back of your hand and the word is "BACK." When you give the reward do not let him come to you but go to him. It is an important point. If you let him come to you, he will start anticipating and want to cheat forward. It will also allow back up training to greater distances.

After he has learned to back up well, you may call him toward you and make him stay at any given point then give him the back up command.

CRAWL

Put him in a down position, holding your hand directly over his head and urge him forward with the leash. Alternately, you will use the words "COME" and "DOWN." The hand signal is moving your hand toward you in a lowered position and the word is "CRAWL."

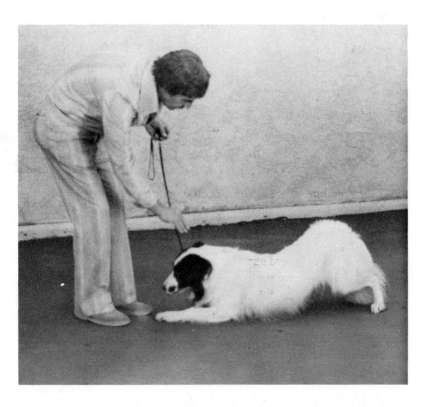

SAY YOUR PRAYERS OR
HIDE YOUR EYES

With the use of the leash teach him to put his feet on the back of a chair and stay. Hold a treat through an opening so he will have to lower his head to get it. At first he will want to take his feet down to get the bite but tell him to "STAY" and withhold the treat until he does. After a time you will be able to direct him to the chair and make a head down motion with your hand. He should stay in position until you come to him with the treat.

ROLL OVER

From the lie down position place your hand under his top front leg and roll him over using the proper words. As the trick is completed give him his reward and praise. Lift his leg a trifle lighter each time until he gets the idea.

Soon he will roll over by either watching your hand motion which remains the same as it was at contact point, or he will react to the words "ROLL OVER."

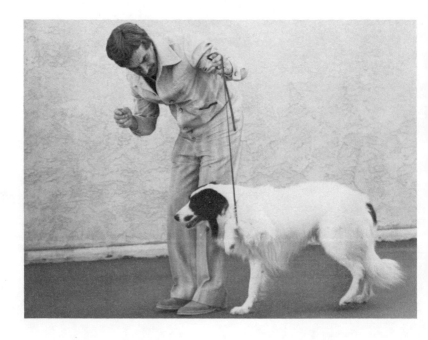

LAME DOG

With leash attached to collar wrap it under dog's leg.
Lift until the leg comes off the ground and urge him to
come to you. At first he will think he can't move or he will
rush too fast. With your help he will soon discover he can
walk with the foot elevated. The hand cue is a quick upward
motion with the hand you favor. Your dog will probably try
to crowd you so be prepared to slow him down by making
him stay after every two or three steps.

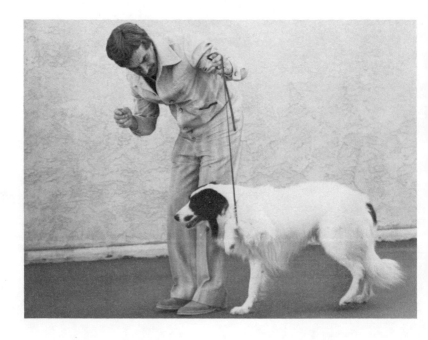

DON'T FORGET THE TREATS

OFF LEASH

By now your dog should not only be pretty well trained, he should have plenty of confidence in both you and himself. He is ready to start working off the leash and at greater distances from you.

I would expect it is now evident that any method you use to persuade your dog to do a certain behavior is okay as long as it does not cause him any discomfort. By using your own imagination, along with a few treats and a lot of praise, there is almost no limit to what your dog can learn.

LAME DOG OFF LEASH

THE CAST IS CHANGING

Meet CHARLEY BROWN and Greg Wallen.
CHARLEY is a mixed terrier. He has been featured on a
number of television shows and motion pictures as well.

JUMP INTO YOUR ARMS

In sequence the pictures demonstrate the procedure. First
have him jump into your lap while you're sitting in a chair.

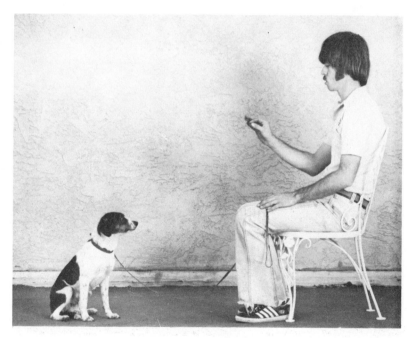

1.

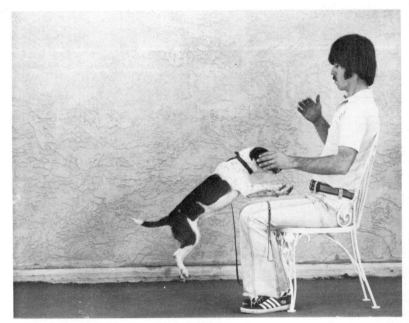

2.

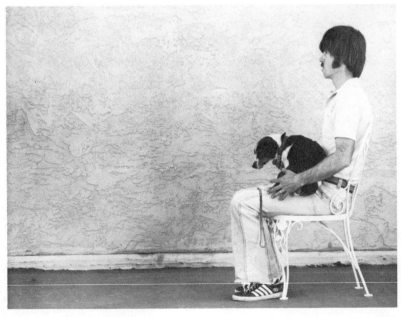

3.

Rise slightly from the chair. Your dog will think you're still sitting and will jump with no hesitation. You might have to train in more gradual stages then the pictures show but it shouldn't take long.

THE STANDING POSITION

Now he'll jump to anyone. All you have to do is pat your chest for a cue.

ALL DOGS SCRATCH FLEAS SOMETIMES

But only a few scratch a flea on cue.

The key to this one is scratching your dog on the chest, side or tummy until he begins to scratch himself. Use the word "SCRATCH" and give him a big reward. Continue doing it this way until he learns the word and will start all by himself. Then for a visual cue scratch your own side until he connects it with the word cue. After that you can use either one. It's a great crowd pleaser.

SNEEZE ON CUE

Rub his nose in this manner. Not too hard. Just enough to make it tickle. Immediately after snap you fingers and say the word "SNEEZE."

You may have to rub his nose or tickle it with a feather a few times to get him started.

When a dog has reached the stage of training yours has, he begins to connect the action of the cues very quickly. Don't forget the reward.

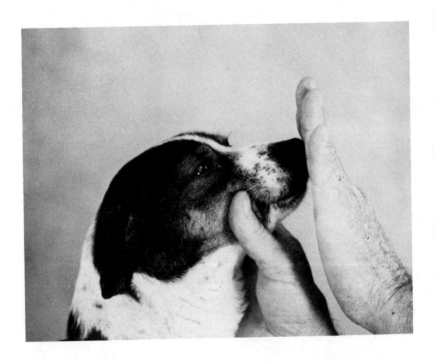

MEET HENRY

HENRY is one of the new stars on the EMERGENCY
television series. He's not really as serious as he looks.
In private life he's a pretty happy-go-lucky kind of fellow.

HENRY is an honest-to-goodness Cinderella dog. One month he was a nobody and the next month he was a television star. He got the job because he was good at doing nothing. Here he is head-to-head with his co-trainer Gary Price. In the next picture Gary is teaching HENRY to yawn. Or is it the other way around?

103

This must be the "wrinkle" for learning to be a success overnight.

"BANDIT" LITTLE HOUSE ON THE PRAIRIE.

HOW TO TRAIN YOUR CAT

For many years it was considered to be impossible to train a house cat. We now know that isn't true. They are highly independent and individualistic as well. They are also very intelligent and if you are in possession of the right key they can learn much obedience and a great number of tricks.

Their behavior patterns are somewhat different from a dog's. In some ways they are not as apt as a dog but in other things they will catch on quicker.

Nature gave dogs certain kinds of advantages for survival and cats other kinds of advantages. In some areas these overlap. In other cases a dog will excel at some behaviors while cats will excel in others.

A cat is very sound oriented so the clicker is an excellent training instrument for it. If you passed up the first of the book concerning birds, go back and review the part dealing with the usage of the clicker.

Cats are responsive to both positive and negative reinforcement. By negative reinforcement we do not mean punishment but only a special kind of a threat one cat gives to another.

POSITIVE REINFORCEMENT

First you should pick up the cat's food dish if you have left one for him to munch whenever he likes.

If you really want to train him with positive reinforcement you must first get him a little bit hungry.

We don't mean to starve him, but you must build a little anxiety for food. At least in the beginning.

Many cats will do all kinds of cute tricks when they feel like it whether they are hungry or not. But if you want him to perform when *you* want him to, he must be looking forward to some kind of treat.

When it's an hour or two past normal feeding time and he is giving some indication of wanting dinner, here's what to do. Hold the dish in your hand. Put a treat or a little bit of his dinner in it. As you offer it to him click the clicker at the same time. When he is finished with that pick up the dish and do the same thing again.

You will be starting to establish a connection between the clicker and food. Get him to follow you and the sound of the clicker before you put the dish down again. For the first session repeat this procedure until his dinner is finished. Each time you might try to get him to come to the clicker sound from a greater distance.

He will learn to recognize that sound in short order. For this purpose it is, in effect, the same thing as calling "kitty kitty!" but it will mean much more than that when he advances in his training.

A WORD OF CAUTION

It is not a good idea to feed the cat from your hand. He may become excited and accidentally grab your finger instead of the treat. When you try to pull away he will dig in harder. It can really hurt.

LEASH TRAINING

It usually takes longer to train a cat to the leash than it does a dog. However, if he learns to lead it makes the training easier, but it isn't essential.

NEGATIVE REINFORCEMENT

The negative reinforcement we use is something the cat understands very well. He understands it by instinct. It is the same "no no" one cat gives to another.

You may have seen one cat hiss and put his paw in another cat's face. Or anything else he wants to give a proper warning.

It's the same kind of thing you will use on him. Because it's part of his nature, he will understand it readily.

If he has a bad habit of jumping on the table or clawing the drapes put your hand over his face and make a hissing sound when you catch him in the act. After you do this a few times, he will begin to believe you mean business.

Eventually, when you see him doing something wrong all you'll need to do is make the hissing sound. He will get off the chair or table, whichever the case may be.

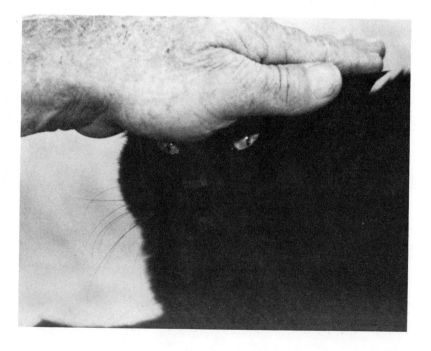

STAY ON CUE

This same hissing sound may be used for making him stay in one position, or to make him stop as you would use STAY with a dog.

To teach him to do this, you may put him on a small table. When he starts to jump off, put your hand in his face and give the HISS cue. When he starts in the other direction, do the same thing. When he knows he will be met with the same negative every time he starts to jump down he will give up and stay in one place.

SIT UP

This one is fairly easy. Hold the dish above his head, coaxing him into the proper position. Push him back down if he tries to stand up.

Remember the clicker. When he has completed the behavior you want, sound the clicker. You should use the verbal "SIT UP." He will be able to learn words just like a dog.

The trick is completed when you can stand a few feet away from him and he will sit up on cue.

ROLL OVER

Push the cat very gently onto his side. At first he will struggle slightly but be firm. When he is reasonably still, roll him over and try to sound the clicker at the same time. He will catch on sooner than you think possible. He might even get to be a pest in his efforts to get your attention along with a treat.

"TIMOTHY"

THE WAVE

If he is trained to STAY this one will be easy. A cat has a natural tendency to reach out for anything he's interested in.

If he knows you have a treat in your hand, he will very quickly reach for it with his paw. When he does, immediately sound the clicker and drop the treat at his feet. Don't offer it to him from your hand.

He will connect the word WAVE and the position of the hand with the reward and set the behavior in his mind.

It appears very showy when you can make him wave from a distance.

JUMP TO THE SHOULDER

Guide him to a chair or to another elevated position where he is able to see the action of your hand when you turn your back to him.

Put the treat in a small container such as a bowl or a cup. Feed him from it until he recognizes it as containing a treat.

The first time or two lean down very close to him with your back to him. Let him see the cup with the treat and persuade him to step to your shoulder to be rewarded.

The next time make him jump a short distance for the treat. This can be extended to leaps of several feet.

THE BIG LEAP

This cat named VELVET loves to ride on the shoulder. He enjoys the ride and will jump from several feet on a direct cue.

It is important to be prepared with enough clothing on your shoulder to protect it. When the cat lands he is forced to extend his claws in order to hold on and keep his balance.

THE CAT RETRIEVE

Like a dog, some cats have a play retrieve. It is not to be depended upon; he will do it only when he feels like it. When you want to show him off, he will most likely have other things he'd rather do.

Your cat can learn to retrieve on cue as can a dog. We must warn you it is more difficult and will take about three weeks if you stay with it for at least one session every day. Here's how it works:

Choose some object like a rolled up piece of cloth or a small ball of yarn. Smear a tiny bit of meat on it and place it in front of your cat. You'd think he'd find it right away but such is not likely to be the case. Most likely you will have to hold it directly to his mouth or nose before he realizes it is food.

When he does discover what it is, place it at his feet. As he starts to lick it off click the clicker and give him a treat from a feed cup. He should remember there was food on the first object and will go back to investigate. The second he puts his nose against it sound the clicker again. Offer the reward again from the cup.

After this has happened a few times he will come to understand there is a connection between touching the object and the reward.

When the connection between the reward and object is
firmly established in his mind you can begin delaying the
click. This will cause a certain amount of frustration.
He will look at you and back at the object, wondering what's
happened. After a time he will start licking the object again
and take it in his mouth to chew. The instant he picks it
up reinforce him with a reward. The next time make him
hold it a little longer.

Now it's time to introduce a shallow container such as you see in the picture.

In the beginning, place the container directly under the cat when he picks the object up. Let him drop it in and reinforce quickly. Keep repeating this until he gets the idea that now the reward is forthcoming because the object is landing inside the container.

You will then move it away only an inch or two until he learns to take the necessary step to drop it in.

After he learns this, things should go a lot faster. Keep extending the distance until you can throw the object any place he can see it and bring it back to the container.

By the time he has come this far, you can substitute your hand for the container.

RATS

Strangely enough a rat is trained almost the same way a cat is trained. There is, however, no negative reinforcement.

They will learn to come to the sound of the clicker, lie down and roll over, sit up, stand on their hind legs and other simple tricks.

We have one trained to climb up a rope to an elevation of fifteen feet where he does a slide for life down a thirty foot cord. Our pal in the picture is named DIRTY RAT.

TRICK HORSES

The technique we have outlined will work very well for training a horse. They usually have a good appetite and will do almost anything for a bit of sugar, apple or carrot. The clicker is a valuable instrument in their training.

We will give you a couple of tips on how to get started, then all you have to do is use your own imagination. The technique you have already learned will work.

TEACH HIM TO SHAKE HIS HEAD NO

Have the clicker and treats ready. Using a pencil or ball point pen, touch your horse on the neck between the head and shoulder. If he doesn't respond the first time by shaking his head, continue to irritate him with it until he shakes his head NO. Quick with the clicker and reward. You'll be surprised at how quickly a horse learns. He will very quickly learn to recognize any visual and verbal cue you care to use.

NOD HIS HEAD YES

Use a light stick and tap him under the chin quickly. He will have a natural tendency to throw his head up. Catch the behavior with the clicker and work the continuing nod by moving the stick up and down.

COUNT

Touch his front ankle with a stick until he lifts his foot — the clicker and payoff.

Training a horse can be good fun. They learn words and visual cues rapidly. They will, in fact learn almost anything if you have time and imagination to invest.

ALL OTHERS

The way you have trained your animal or bird will work with almost any other kind of animal or fowl.

We have tried to give you all the ingredients in a simple and straightforward manner.

With your little clicker you have all you need to compete with the behavioral psychologists. If you have developed an understanding with your pet this is an advantage.

Good luck. We hope by now you agree with us that loving and understanding your pet is the best way to train him and keep him as a friend.

A TRAINED RAVEN